THE PATIENT

WHO THOUGHT

HE WAS DEAD

AND OTHER PSYCHOLOGICAL STORIES

THE PATIENT

WHO THOUGHT

HE WAS DEAD

AND OTHER PSYCHOLOGICAL STORIES

DR. JOHN KARAHALIS

gatekeeper press™

Columbus, Ohio

The Patient Who Thought He Was Dead: and Other Psychological Stories

Published by Gatekeeper Press
2167 Stringtown Rd, Suite 109
Columbus, OH 43123-2989
www.GatekeeperPress.com

ISBN (hardcover): 9781662902093
ISBN (paperback): 9781662902109
eISBN: 9781662902116

Library of Congress Control Number: 2020940172

Contents

Introduction

The stories contained in this book are all real stories that have occurred over my thirty-five years of working as a psychologist in a variety of settings, from preschool programs to psychiatric hospitals. Some of the stories are humorous, some are tragic. All names and any identifying information have been changed to protect the confidentiality of the aforementioned, but the stories are as accurate as I can recall them.

The purpose of this book is not to stigmatize or stereotype those with cognitive, behavioral, or mental disorders but to realize that their stories are very often not atypical after all. We can all empathize that our life, no matter how difficult, may pale in comparison to what many others in our world have to contend with on a daily basis.

As I often tell my college students: *"I hope the worst day of your life has already been played out in your life. I hope the worst thing that can ever happen to you has already happened. But please try to remember that the worst day of your life, no matter how horrific it may have been, might be someone else's best day of their life. For even though you have dealt with difficulty and tragedy in your life, you still have a warm bed to sleep in, a roof over your head, and people who love and care for you. That's not a guarantee for everyone. For some of those living today, each day is a struggle to survive. Where to sleep, food to eat, avoiding being victimized by society."*

I'd like to dedicate this book to all of the survivors, past and present, who, despite the struggles, made it through the storm and came out the other side stronger and wiser.

Be Careful What You Say

I was conducting a group counseling class for students with cerebral palsy who were expecting a sibling soon. The general purpose was to talk about what to expect with a newborn baby, as most of these students were only children up to now. Tommy was a five-year-old with cerebral palsy and in a wheelchair. His mother was expecting another baby in a few months, and Tommy was aware of his soon-to-be sibling. Tommy told me he asked his mother, "Will the baby have cerebral palsy too?"

Tommy's mother responded, "God, I hope not!"

Tommy wanted to know why his mother said that.

We All Can Make a Difference

Mike was an adult with spastic quadriplegic cerebral palsy. He had no functional use of his arms or legs. The engineering department where I worked was able to design a motorized wheelchair that he was able to use with the limited movement of his right hand. One day, while traveling in his wheelchair near his home, Mike saw a car on the side of the road and a young mother holding a baby, looking distressed.

Mike wheeled up to this woman and, without hesitation, asked her, "Is there anything I can do to help you?" Mike did not let his physical challenges diminish his need to help others.

The Girlfriend

Dan was a teenager who saw me for counseling in a school for those with physical challenges. Dan not only had spastic quadriplegia but could not speak and, due to his severe CP, would drool constantly. He could only communicate using a head pointer, which was a converted helmet with a small metal bar that protruded from the top. He would spell out his thoughts on a communication board that contained the alphabet and some common phrases such as *yes, no, how are you,* etc.

During one particular session, Dan spelled out for me, "I have a girlfriend!"

I replied, "Is she a student here at the school?"

Immediately, Dan's face turned from smiling to angry. His face got red and he moved from side to side in his wheelchair. He carefully spelled out on his communication device, "What makes you think she has cerebral palsy too!"

As it turned out, he was correct. She was a neighborhood girl who had known Dan since childhood. She spent hours with Dan each day and enjoyed his company and he, hers. They talked about everything—school, sports, the future, life. In Dan's mind as well as hers, they were boyfriend and girlfriend.

Sal's Story

I was a newly assigned psychologist working in a hospital setting for patients with psychiatric disorders. It was my first day, and I was dressed in my professional best. The administrator on the admissions ward asked me to see Sal. He gave no other details.

I walked onto the admissions ward of twenty-five middle-aged men and scoped the ward. Suddenly, about a third of the patients started getting up and walking slowly towards me. At first, I thought it unusual and then quickly became concerned that I was in the middle of a zombie epidemic. I held my ground, not wanting to look frightened or concerned.

As these patients got to within a few feet of me, they all seemed to speak nearly in unison.

"Are you a lawyer? Are you a lawyer? You gotta get me out of here. Are you a lawyer?"

I replied, "Sorry, I'm a psychologist. By the way, do any of you know who Sal is?" Most of them turned and walked away.

One patient said, "I think he is in the corner over there."

As I got closer, other patients pointed in the direction of the corner of the ward. Sal was sitting alone, hunched up in a fetal position. He was mumbling to himself over and over like a mantra. "I lost my job. My wife left me. I have no reason to live."

I introduced myself and asked him if he would speak to me in my office. He joined me. Then, slowly sitting down, he repeated the mantra I had heard on the ward, "I lost my job. My wife left me. I have no reason to live." I then learned his story.

Sal was a very successful real estate salesman financially, doing very well, living in the suburbs with his wife and two teenage daughters. One day he didn't feel like going to work. He didn't call the office, and later that day, they called him at home. "Sal, are you coming in today?"

He replied, "No," and hung up the phone. The following day, the same occurred. He did not go to work and did not call the office.

When they called him, they repeated their question. "Sal, are you coming in today? Are you sick?"

He answered, "Leave me alone," and hung up the phone. This went on the whole week and into the following weeks.

Finally, the real estate agency told Sal they could not hold his position open if he was not coming back to work and not giving a plausible explanation. So, they let him go.

Meanwhile, Sal's wife was trying to find out what was wrong with her husband. "Sal, you need to see a doctor. Sal, what's wrong with you? We have no money coming in and you lost your job. You need to see someone."

But Sal refused to discuss the matter and stayed mostly in bed throughout the day, talking little to his wife and children. Finally, faced with no other option, Sal's wife told him she was leaving with the girls to go to her mother's house. Then Sal made a suicide attempt, which resulted in him getting admitted to the hospital.

What Sal experienced is clinical depression. This is not to be confused with the typical depression most of us experience due to the daily issues life brings us. Psychologist and researcher Otto Ronk called depression "the common cold of psychopathology." In other words, we all get depressed sometime in our life and some more often than others. Some depression, like a cold, is annoying but does not prevent you from going to work and continuing your everyday activities. Other colds are so bad they may make it difficult to get out of bed and cause you to just want to sleep the day away.

But Sal had clinical depression. Everything he told me was true, but the order it occurred in was the difference. He first became depressed, followed by losing his job, family, and finally, nearly his life.

I worked with Sal for over three years as an inpatient. He was not responding to treatment. He told me on more than one occasion, "I am never going to leave this place. I am going to die here." But I refused to allow Sal to accept that.

I told him, "No, Sal. You *will* leave here, and you will get your life back again." Privately, I wasn't so sure. But I knew if I gave up on Sal and he picked up on that, he would never leave.

It took three long years, but Sal eventually got well enough to leave. I then lost contact with Sal until six months later, when a new sports car pulled up to my building. It was Sal, come to see me. He told me he was back working in real estate and doing well. He was seeing a psychologist weekly and had a doctor to monitor his medication.

When I asked how his family was, he said he and his wife were not back together, but he got to see his daughters regularly. Apparently, his wife was not so sure he would not get sick again. I wished him well and told him to make sure he took his medication and continued with counseling. He assured me that he would. He thanked me for never giving up on him.

I never saw Sal again after that day. That was one of my success stories. I had many over the years that did not end so well. But I'll never forget Sal.

Billy's Story

Billy was an eighteen-year-old senior in a school for those with physical limitations. His gross motor skills were fine, but his fine motor skills were limited. In addition, Billy had a severe stuttering problem, more appropriately referred to today as an expressive articulation disorder. When asked how he was, he replied, "FFFFFFFFFFFFFine."

Despite his severe difficulties in easily expressing himself, he was accepted by all his classmates and was never made fun of. Billy also had a secret skill. He could sing wonderfully without missing a beat. At first, teachers and peers in his district school thought he was faking his stuttering. However, this was not a ruse. Each year the school would have a talent show and Billy would sing. And not only sing, but sing very well and in tune.

One evening, at home, Billy stayed up late watching a program on TV. His parents were asleep. He heard a commotion outside his house and noticed two men trying to steal his neighbor's car. Without waking his parents, Billy ran outside and feverishly banged on his neighbor's door.

The owner answered and asked, "Billy, what's wrong?

Billy replied, "They'rrrrrrrrrrrrrrrrrrre."

The homeowner again asked, "Billy, is everything okay?"

Again, Billy replied, "They'rrrrrrrrrrrrrrrrrrrrrre."

Concerned, the homeowner said again, "Billy, what is it?"

Finally, Billy knew exactly what to do. He sang his response. "They're stealing your car! They're stealing your car! You better come on out now, before they go far. They're gonna drive it away. They're gonna drive it away. It will be gone if you just stay."

The owner rushed out just in time to stop the two kids that were about to jump-start the car for a joy ride.

David, the Patient Who Thought He Was Dead

David was a patient I had in a psychiatric hospital. He was diagnosed with schizophrenia, the most disabling form of mental illness. David had a strong delusion that he was dead. Now, how do you conduct therapy with someone who is dead?

I would say, "David, you're not dead."

He would say, "I am dead."

I would reply, "But David, you are sitting across from me having a cup of coffee. How can you be dead?"

He would insist, "I am dead."

No matter what I tried to get David to see he was alive, nothing worked. I was running out of ideas. Finally, after weeks of frustration, I casually said to David, not even thinking about it, "So, David, do dead men bleed?"

And David replied, "No, I guess dead men don't bleed."

As soon as he said that, I called the nurses' station and asked the nurse to sterilize a needle and come to my office ASAP. When she arrived, I asked David to open his hand, which he did. I asked the nurse to prick his pinkie finger with the needle. A drop of blood came to the surface of his skin.

I then said confidently, "Look, David, you're bleeding. You're bleeding. What does that say to you? What does that tell you?"

His reply was quick and to the point. "Well, I guess it means that ... DEAD MEN **DO** BLEED."

Animals Falling from the Sky

Many psychiatrists are foreign-born and have areas of specialty different from psychiatry. Apparently, it is easier to become licensed in psychiatry in the USA than in any other field of medicine if you are a physician from another country. As a result, the hospital where I worked had psychiatrists who were surgeons in their home country. Or cardiologists, anesthesiologists, and neurologists.

There was one doctor who was born in India and had only been practicing in the USA for a few years. Although qualified to practice, she was not familiar with American colloquialisms. For example, if a patient said, "I don't feel so hot," the doctor took it literally and raised the thermostat in her office.

I had one of the doctor's patients for counseling and was going through his chart. The doctor had written that my patient had severe hallucinations. In fact, she wrote that my patient was seeing animals falling from the sky. Not that the patient was without issues, but hallucinations were not a problem I was aware of.

I asked the patient if he recalled speaking to this doctor recently, and he did. I asked him if he told the doctor that he saw animals falling from the sky. I said,

"Well, that's what she wrote in your chart." He was upset and confused. I said, "Think about that day. What was going on?"

He said, "Well, I was talking to the doc, and it was pouring outside. I pointed out the window and said, 'Hey, doc, look out the window. It's raining cats and dogs.'"

I had to see the doctor to explain what the patient meant and correct the report.

Zack from the Planet Zircon

When I began working in a psychiatric hospital for the first time I primarily worked on admissions and later moved to a chronic building. Many of those patients were 'long-timers.' It was not unusual to have patients with 20 or more years of continuous placement (a nicer way of stating than 'confinement').

Zack was one of these older patients. When I first met him, to me, he was like a grandpa anyone would want. Intelligent, funny and able to carry on a coherent conversation. I began to wonder why Zack was in this facility and perhaps he was some homeless person stumbling into the building years ago for the warm bed and food and has been fooling everyone ever since. Then one particular session Zack told me he had a secret.

"You know I am an alien."

"Huh? From another country?"

"No, from the planet Zircon."

Now, I should have realized where I was and where this person was talking to me but my first reaction was somewhat unprofessional to say the least.

"Are you shitting me?"

Then Zack went on in excruciating detail of the vast solar system and planet he was from and how he is in the hospital to gain knowledge of the human race to prepare the Zircons to populate the planet Earth. This occurred after a long and stressful week and I should have had more coffee in me but for a fleeting moment he almost had me convinced.

I finally realized something about mental illness that I didn't really learn in school. Mentally ill people are not necessarily mentally ill 24/7. Many can be as clear and coherent as you or I. Unlike other types of challenges such as cognitive, limitations and physical challenges, which remain relatively consistent. A mentally ill person can be no different than the rest of society the majority of the time but can be completely incoherent on any given day. This day was Zack's day and the reason why he was living where he was. I think?

Gary the Gambler

Gary liked to gamble. He used to read the paper for the track posting every day and would bet on horses. Little did I know he was doing this all while being an inpatient in a psychiatric hospital. One day he asked if he could use my office phone to call his mother. I obliged. I heard him say to the person on the other end, "Yeah, it's the G man. I wanna put five on the nose on Mothers' Helper in the third race at Belmont."

Once I knew I had been had, that was the last time he used my phone.

On another occasion, Gary told me how he always could pick a winner. I asked him how he could be so sure. I opened the daily paper and he scanned the horses. "It's the 'I' horse," he said confidently.

I said, "How can you be so sure?"

He responded, "Because I always win."

Trips into the Community

On occasion we would be able to take some of the residents from the psychiatric hospital into the community for movies, bowling or parks. The highlight of those days was going to McDonald's or some other fast food establishment for lunch. Many of the long-timers rarely got to see anything but the dreary building and weed-infested grounds of the large complex. But before we would depart I would turn to these patients prior to boarding the bus and dispatch my orders like a Drill Sargent.

"We are going into town to see a (movie, bowling, fishing, park, etc.) *I know you are all considered mental patients but that's only at the hospital. In the community you are not mental patients and I expect you to act like everyone else. That means no making any wild claims like you are a famous celebrity or historical figure. Begging strangers for money, using the nearest tree as a bathroom or asking someone having lunch if they are going to finish their meal. For if you do, it will be a long time before you will be allowed to go on a trip again.*"

I have to admit. These individuals all behaved like perfect ladies and gentlemen for the full duration in the community. I never had a problem. However, once we departed the bus and entered the hospital, upon our return, all of their symptoms re-appeared. Were they faking it? No. Even the most seriously mentally impaired person has the ability to control their behavior and atypical thought processes for a short duration if the incentive is strong enough. Sadly, even with the benefit of intensive therapy and medication, when prescribed, success rates are never 100%.

Wheelchair Island

I conducted weekly group counseling sessions with ten high school students who had varying degrees of cerebral palsy. Some had functional use of their arms and some were totally immobilized from the neck down, unable to use verbal language. My supervisor came up with the premise of that day's session. "Tell them the government has created Wheelchair Island where they can move and live among others just like themselves, totally removed from society, in a world designed for only those in wheelchairs."

I was reluctant, but being still on probation as a new employee, I felt obligated to do as my supervisor said. So I proceeded with what I was told to say. "Guess what, everyone? The United States government has just decided to create a special place for those in wheelchairs. It's going to be called Wheelchair Island. Here, on an island off the coast of Florida, a specially designed place will be made. All wheelchair-accessible, of course. Ramps everywhere, wider doorways, and wheelchair-accessible sinks, bathrooms, and bedrooms. Round-the-clock aides to attend to your every need. You never have to leave. But there is one catch: you must stay on the island, and no one who is not in a wheelchair can live there. Doesn't that sound great?"

I suddenly saw the group respond, and not in a positive way. Some shouted, "Are you serious?" Some literally bounced in their wheelchairs, and some got visibly red in the face with an anger directed to me that I had never witnessed before.

Finally, one of the group members spoke the sentiment that all of the students must have been thinking. "Why do you think that I want to be isolated from society, surrounded by only people like me until the end of my time? This is discrimination. This is isolating people who are different. This is ridiculous and wrong."

I had to quickly say that this was not true and it was just an exercise in understanding how even though we have our differences, be it race, culture, religion, or physical limitations, we have more in common than we don't. I also told them the idea of today's session was not mine and threw my supervisor under the bus. I had to work with those students the following week.

Profanity Frank

Frank was an adolescent I worked with in a psychiatric hospital. Among his issues was the inability to speak a sentence without using profanity. The staff and nurses grew tired of the sewage that emanated from his mouth. Other patients also did not take kindly to his nonstop vulgarity train. It became my responsibility to see what I could do to decrease the frequency of his inappropriate utterances.

I asked Frank, "What can I do to get you to stop cursing? It's very inappropriate and is causing problems on the ward with the other patients and the staff." Being experienced in reinforcement behavioral therapy, I asked him if there was anything I could offer as an incentive to stop this behavior.

Thinking he was about to ask for some ridiculous thing like a Lamborghini, yacht, or a million dollars, I was surprised to hear him say, "How about a two-liter bottle of Coca-Cola?"

The following day, I was ready for my behavioral program for Frank. I told him he had to avoid using any profanity or four-letter words from 8 a.m. (when I arrived at work) till noon. If he could do that, the soda was his.

The following day, the program began. I arrived at work and saw Frank. I greeted him with, "Good morning."

He greeted me with, "Fuck you."

I replied, "Sorry, Frank, not today."

The next day, the same thing occurred. Each day, one of the staff or I would report that Frank "screwed up again." The bottle of Coke remained untouched in my office.

About a week later, I was working in my office, writing up one of the many reports I needed to catch up on, and lost track of time. I noticed Frank pacing outside my office, but he didn't seem to want to see me. I had not gotten any feedback from the staff about Frank that day and just continued with what I was doing.

Finally, Frank peeked his head in my office and asked, "Excuse me. What time is it?"

Looking at my trusty Timex watch, I answered, "12:05."

He then smiled and said, "Fuck you. Give me my soda."

Now, my first instinct was to tell Frank he was not getting that soda, but I quickly realized he knew exactly what he was doing and was testing me. If I did not give him the bottle, I would lose all credibility with him and he would never trust me again. So, I handed him the soda and said, "Okay, Frank, you got me. You win. Tomorrow I will bring in another bottle of Coke for you, but this time you have to keep from cursing till 5 p.m."

Play Therapy

Play therapy is a form of therapeutic treatment with children. It is exactly what it sounds like. While working in an elementary school for emotionally disturbed children, I spent the majority of my day on the floor, playing with markers, crayons, toy cars, trucks, dolls, and action figures. I also had family puppets of all ethnicities. This would allow the child to create his or her family and in doing so, I would gain insight into the family structure and dynamics.

My office was fairly large, so I was able to play a good number of full-court Nerf basketball games. Suffice it to say, I came home looking more like the last runner finishing a marathon than a school psychologist. One thing I learned early in my career about children: they are very open about their feelings once they begin to know you and trust you.

Most of the teachers and administrators didn't initially comprehend what I was doing. I think they thought I was either stealing the school's money by playing games all day or revisiting my childhood. The following stories occurred at this time.

The Boy That Wouldn't Talk

Adam was a seven-year-old that I was asked to see. There was not much history about him other than that he had been sent to this school for not participating in the classroom and being selectively mute. I saw him for counseling twice a week and we spent the first three months playing basketball, Connect Four, and checkers. Win or lose, his expression stayed the same. I asked him no questions, and he offered no responses.

Finally, during a really good competitive game of Nerf basketball, Adam made his first statement to me. "Why does my daddy hit my mommy and make her cry?" The wound had finally been lanced, and a new chapter in this child's life was revealed.

Carlos and his Mothers

Working in a middle school you are interacting with students transitioning into adolescents and all the hormonal changes that go along with that transformation. You never know what is there to greet you on a daily basis. Relationships and peer-related events that usually seem trivial only a few years later are all magnified in middle school. It's not a surprise that eating disorders are so prevalent today in adolescent girls.

There was a young adolescent who had been living in State residential centers since childhood. His anger from a horrific past was justified and as a result he was never successful in staying in a foster care home for long. His anger, rooted in his past, somehow sabotaged each placement. Children in state residential facilities are like kennels. Everyone wants a puppy. Older dogs and older children are not as appealing to those willing to take on a foster child. Carlos however finally lucked out. There was a same-sex couple who were willing to take on the challenge. They understood the baggage Carlos had in his past and were prepared to give him a loving, supportive home. And they did as promised! I recall his teacher telling me they were the best parents she ever had. They would come to open school night, were always available to come to school if there was an issue with Carlos, followed up on both the curriculum and behavioral programs we implemented to keep Carlos on the straight and narrow. All was going well until this one particular day.

Carlos got into a verbal altercation with another student. They were getting louder and the insults began to fly.

"You're stupid"

"No you're stupid."

"You're ugly."

"You're uglier."

Then the insults got personal. The other student uttered the words many students have used to insult a peer. In my parents' time it would be something like; *"Your mother wears army boots"* or something close. But what Carlos heard brought out a reaction even his adversary was not expecting to see.

The classmate shouted out *"Your mother's gay."* Now I knew for a fact that this student did not know Carlos's home environment. It was just a moronic statement that kids would say to each other when they ran out of anything else to say. But Carlos didn't know that. He took it personally. Thinking that this classmate knew his home environment and in his mind feeling that his "mothers" were just insulted by that statement, he pummeled this peer, and as a result three staff members had to intervene to hold him back from not doing more damage. The student on the receiving end of Carlos's anger could not comprehend why he was so angry. And no one ever told him.

Drug-Dealing Dan

Daniel was an eight-year-old boy who lived in a drug-infested high-crime neighborhood where gangs and drug dealing were as common as the broken beer bottles on the street. He came to me due to aggressive behavior in his district program that resulted in him being placed in a special program for emotionally disturbed students.

Daniel was always appropriate with me, his counselor, and would openly discuss his anger and frustrations. One day, I asked Daniel what he would like to be when he grew up.

Without any hesitation, Daniel replied, "A drug dealer."

I asked him why he would want to be a drug dealer as that is not only against the law but a dangerous thing to do. I explained he might eventually wind up in jail or get himself killed. His reply was poignant and, to some extent, very logical. "At least for a while, I will have a cool car, lots of clothes, a bunch of girlfriends, and tons of money to buy anything I want."

Sleeping Arrangements

Several of our students in the schools I worked at came from economically impoverished neighborhoods. Many of these families were new immigrants and came to this country knowing little language and with only the money in their pockets. Not unlike my ancestors and perhaps many of your ancestors did. Large families often had to make do with limited bedroom or sleeping options. One of my students moved to Long Island from a South American country to escape crime and poverty that made every day another day for survival. Public schools do not get involved in immigration status. All children must attend.

This student, Pablo, lived in a two bedroom apartment with his mother and two teenage sisters. Pablo was 10 years old. His sisters slept in one of the bedrooms, Pablo, in the remaining one with his mother. During a lunch period Pablo and other classmates were talking about where they live, if they have siblings and if they have their own room. When it came time for Pablo to talk he revealed that he had been sleeping in the same room as his mother.

"Why?" they asked.

"Because my two older sisters are in the other bedroom."

"You have two beds in that room?"

"No," Pablo replied. *"I sleep in the same big bed as my mother."*

Almost in unison the other students said in amazement:

"That's sick. You shouldn't do that. That's wrong."

There was nothing sinister or inappropriate, or wrong going on here. The bedroom arrangement was due to necessity. Such an arrangement may be typical in South America and large families, but to his American peers they saw it differently. Pablo felt embarrassed and thought his friends saw something he didn't. In actuality, it was his classmates that needed to learn more about the world outside of their own homes.

Role Reversals

I've worked with children from infancy through young adulthood. No, I didn't conduct therapy with infants, in case you were wondering. However, I did evaluate them with adaptive tests and developmental screenings. Not unlike what a pediatrician would do. This gave me information on the developmental milestones, both cognitive and physical, that I needed to know to determine the level of function a child was at. As any parent knows, there is a major difference between what a six-month-old and an eighteen-month-old can do.

One memorable recollection is a pretty little five-year-old girl named Ashley. Blonde hair and blue eyes. She looked like a kid from a Disney kid show. But looks can be deceiving. She was removed from her kindergarten program for assaultive and verbally aggressive behavior. I had my work cut out for me.

I learned early on that Ashley liked to play teacher. She would say to me, "I wanna be a teacher."

I said that that was a wonderful idea when she grew up. However, she meant now, during the session. So, Ashley would spend most sessions teaching me how to read and write, and I learned all my colors and shapes. Occasionally, I would purposely make a mistake in identifying a shape or color, and her retort was quick and to the point. "That's wrong. Are you stupid?"

I would quickly apologize and correct my error.

She said, "Don't make that mistake again."

My first inclination was that her teacher was especially punitive, but I quickly investigated and was confident that was not the case.

As each session progressed, Ashley became more demanding and angry with me. She also insisted that I sit in a child's chair, and she in my larger leather office chair behind my desk. As she towered over me in my little chair, she would begin to berate me. "Do your homework. Stop looking at me. Don't talk."

One particular day she was so angry with me that she asked me to go stand in the corner of my office. Of course, I obliged, but I also responded, "I don't want to stand in the corner."

She replied, "Shut up and don't talk."

I had a small wastepaper basket in my office. When Ashley followed up with, "Go stand in the garbage can because you are garbage," I realized the issue here was significant, and family therapy and a child protective case might be a potential concern.

Ashley came closer to me as I was trying to whimper in my best child's voice, "Why are you so mad at me?"

Standing behind me, Ashley raised her little finger and pointed at me as I was standing in my garbage can, saying, "You're bad, you're bad, you're bad."

At that exact moment, the principal of the program opened my office door and saw me in the garbage can with this little girl screaming at me. How I didn't lose my job that day was a miracle. It took a great deal of explaining what play therapy was to the principal.

As a follow-up, Ashley's mother was a single mother with a newborn and Ashley at home. Although verbally abusive, she was not physically assaultive with Ashley. Though not a perfect parent by any means, the mother was overwhelmed. The social worker and I were able to get home-care assistance and counseling for her as I continued with Ashley at school. Things got better for the family.

Not Nominated for Parents of the Year

In many years of working in school settings, I have seen my share of strange stories involving parents and their children. Some resulted in reports to Child Protective Services, and some should have but did not. The following are actual cases I have been involved in.

Peter and the Point Sheets

In an elementary school for behaviorally involved children, we had a program whereby students would receive points on a point sheet they carried for appropriate behavior. Points included things like entering the classroom and taking your seat, not leaving the classroom without permission, avoiding using profanity, respecting peers and staff, and attempting and/or completing in-class assignments. The points were awarded every half-hour period. Five points on five specific factors could earn a student a maximum of thirty points per day.

If a student earned twenty-five points or more, he would move towards a higher level. Each level would earn more rewards and extra privileges such as reward gym, computer time, and school store, where students could trade in whatever points they earned for reinforcers like food items, toys, costume jewelry, and sports equipment. Every student had the opportunity to earn something. Students were required to take home the point sheet daily and have it signed by their parents to be returned the following day.

One youngster, Peter, a seven-year-old, bought into the reward system as the majority of the students did. However, a problem always occurred when Peter did not earn the maximum points possible, thirty. In fact, he refused to get on the bus if he didn't earn thirty points. The teachers and I literally had to strap him in his seat and ask the bus driver to pull away, as Peter would attempt to get off the bus if it was not moving.

I had my suspicions that there was an issue, so I called home. A man answered, and I introduced myself as the school psychologist and said I was calling about Peter. The man replied, "I am his father. What's this all about?"

I asked him if he was familiar with the point-sheet behavior program we used at school. Sounding a little perturbed, he replied, "Yes, I am very familiar with your program."

I then informed him about the difficulty we had with Peter getting on the bus if he did not reach the maximum points allowed for the day and explained that we had tried to let Peter know that twenty-five points or more per day still earned him the next level of our reward system. "Can you please let Peter know that he does not have to earn a perfect score each day?" I requested.

Peter's father replied, "Well, that might be okay for the other kids at your school, but I am a veteran, and in the military, we don't accept any less than the best. If thirty is the best, that's what he has to earn. Otherwise, it's straight to bed after dinner. No TV, no video games, no computer time."

I tried to explain to Peter's father in my most respectful voice, "But sir, he is doing very well overall, and we would like him to know that he is earning towards his next level in our reward system. We don't expect perfection at his age."

But there was no compromise from the father. I could not convince him of how the program reward system worked. So what to do?

This was certainly not a case for CPS. The father was punitive and very rigid, but there was no evidence of any abuse that I could report. Parents have the right to discipline children as they see fit, as long as it does not result in physical harm or dangerous consequences to the child.

Here was my dilemma. The child would not accept points below the maximum of thirty. The father would not accept points that did not add up to a perfect score. From the school and program's point of view, twenty-five or more was sufficient to earn toward the next level. I gave it a great deal of thought and decided how to proceed.

Starting the next day, if Peter earned twenty-five or more points for the day, the point sheet would be changed to thirty. From our perspective, and for all intents and purposes, he did earn his reward. However, this was not a blank check. If Peter earned less than twenty-five points for the day, the points would remain as earned, as the consequence for earning less than twenty-five points was the same for all students.

As a result, there were fewer occurrences of Peter refusing to get on the bus. I expect his father was happy to see Peter's improvement, and the school was able to continue with the program with little adjustment.

Night-Owl Nicky

Nicky was a second-grade student. As his assigned counselor, I met with him once a week. After a few weeks of nonsignificant issues, Nicky had a secret to tell me. "Guess what?" he said. "On TV, there is a channel that has naked people doing all kinds of things."

When I asked about what kinds of things, he began to describe sexual positions I didn't know until I was nearly an adult. I asked if his parents knew about this, and Nicky said, "Don't tell, but they're asleep. It's on after they go to bed."

Apparently, Nicky had found his way to the Playboy channel while channel surfing. When I later called Nicky's mother, I asked her if she knew that Nicky stayed up late at night and watched TV.

His mother responded, "Oh yes. He's a night owl." I asked if she knew what Nicky watched. She replied, "I guess Cartoon Network?"

I told her, "Not exactly," and proceeded to explain that Nicky would be the most knowledgeable second grader about sexuality in the county. Embarrassed, his parents quickly blocked the channel. Problem solved, but the cat was out of the bag.

Sleepy Sam

Sam was a well-liked nine-year-old. Never a problem, except I started getting reports that Sam was sleeping in some of his classes. It happened two times one week and three times the next. In fact, he was so out of it on the third occasion of the second week that the school nurse was called to take vital signs, thinking Sam might have gotten his hands on some sort of chemical substance. All vitals checked out.

The nurse was going to call Sam's mother, but I asked if she would allow me to interview Sam first. When I brought Sam into my office, I asked him why he was so sleepy. He looked at me and asked, "Why?"

"Because you can't learn in school if you're asleep."

"Well," he said, "sometimes my mom wakes me up and I have to go with her to visit one of her friends." I did not respond and let him continue. "Mom tells me to watch TV on the couch and she goes in the bedroom to talk to a man friend. Then, after an hour, she comes out, and we go home."

Rather than pursue this any further, I called the mother after Sam left. "Mrs. S, are you aware that Sam is having trouble staying awake in class?"

"He is?"

"In fact, we had trouble waking him in his history class today. I spoke to him, and you're not going to believe this wild story he told me! He said that a few times a week, you wake him up and he has to go with you to visit one of your man friends and he watches TV while you talk to this man in his bedroom for an hour. Isn't that the craziest thing you ever heard?"

"Oh it's crazy, all right."

"You know, Mrs. S, Sam needs his sleep if he is going to do well in school. That's very important. I hope you will see that he gets all the sleep he needs from now on."

"Okay, I will."

Now, to be honest, I was never 100 percent sure what exactly was going on in that bedroom and could not accuse the mother of any inappropriate behavior, but I did narrow it down to a few ideas, none positive. However, I think she knew that I knew. Suffice it to say, there was no repeat of Sam falling asleep in class after that phone call.

Alienating Allen

Allen was a thirteen-year-old student who was placed in a program for emotionally affected students. The main issue was he would self-isolate and not interact with his peers. Allen was also obese and, as a result, was an easy target for the bullies in the school. However, the bullies were very careful not to intimidate Allen when teachers or staff were able to observe. Apparently, this went on for weeks.

Allen came to my attention when his teacher alerted me of the fact that no students would sit anywhere near him. In fact, students were complaining that Allen *stank*.

I invited Allen to my office. One thing was for sure; he didn't smell like roses. I had to admit, the stench was overwhelming.

Allen told me that he was tired of all the kids picking on him because of his size. He said they were also throwing spitballs at him and physically threatening and intimidating him, all behind the school staff's back. Afraid to report this and the retaliating that would ensue, Allen found a very effective solution to this problem. He made himself so offensive-smelling that no student would get within ten feet of him, thereby giving him the security and space needed to keep those students from affecting him.

As unfortunate as that was, the method Allen used was even more traumatic. What he would do was intentionally defecate on himself (known as encopresis) as a way to keep others away. I have to admit, it *was* very effective, as no one would dare go near him. I called his mother later and was surprised to learn that Allen had also used this technique in his past school.

The school was able to monitor the bullies and keep a closer eye on the classes, but Allen continued this behavior. His mother was eventually asked to have Allen bring an extra set of clothing to school each day so he could change when this occurred.

As his assigned counselor, it was my responsibility to accompany Allen to the shower in the gym and wait outside as Allen bathed and changed into fresh clothing. He had a plastic bag in which to take home his soiled clothes. The following day, the routine would often reoccur. On some occasions, it happened more than one time a day, and Allen went home still wearing soiled clothes.

Due to the safety and hygienic aspects of this issue, Allen was put on home instruction and the district had to assign teachers to go to his home. Reports came back that the home smelled like s***. It was difficult to get the same teachers to report to the home daily.

It's hard to imagine that a child would resort to such extreme measures to avoid being bullied, but as you may have read, students have taken their own lives due to bullying.

There are three people involved in bullying.

1. The bully,
2. the person being bullied,
3. and the witness to the bullying who does not try to intervene, stop it, or at least report it to someone such as a staff person, if it occurs at a school, or to a responsible adult if it happens elsewhere.

Home-Alone Henry

Henry was a ten-year-old student who was classified with a learning disability. He was a relatively good student despite his struggles. There was never a reported problem with Henry up until one particular Friday when some of his classmates complained to his teacher that he smelled awful. In fact, a few of the teachers reported that he seemed to be wearing the exact same clothes all week. I needed to investigate.

I brought Henry into my office. He sat down. The odor was pungent, to say the least. "Gee, Henry, you really like that shirt and those pants, don't you?" I said.

His reply was, "What do you mean?"

"Well, Henry, some of the teachers think this is the fourth day in a row you are wearing those clothes. Why don't you wear something else?"

"I can't," he replied.

"And why is that?"

"Because all my other clothes are dirty."

"Can't your mom wash them or bring them to the laundromat?"

"No."

"Why?"

"Because she's not home."

"Where is your mom?" I inquired.

"She had to leave to visit my aunt far away."

I began to become more concerned. "So who is with you at home now?"

"Just me and my sister."

"And how old is your sister?"

"Five," he said.

I knew I had to act quickly, so I made a call to the police department as well as CPS. As it turned out, Henry was pretty accurate. His mother had gone to take care of her sister, leaving Henry and his sister home alone. She asked a neighbor who lived in the apartment above them to make sure that they got on the school bus and got back in the house at the end of the day. The mother told the neighbor that she left plenty of cold cuts and peanut butter and jelly for the kids and that they would be fine. She told the neighbor she would only be gone a few days.

When the mother eventually arrived home, she found her children were gone, and there was a note on her door to call the police. The neighbor told the mother they were safe, but CPS and the police had taken the children into temporary protective custody. The police and CPS explained to the mother the danger the kids could have gotten into and read her the riot act.

The mother was able to get Henry and his sister back after pleading and promising to never leave them home alone again, with periodic visits to follow by CPS.

The one saving grace for the mother was that she had alerted her neighbor to, at a minimum, watch the kids get on and off the bus. Otherwise, she surely would have lost custody entirely.

Mark's Mother

Mark was a middle-school adolescent who had spent most of his life in foster care. Mark's biological mother had a drug and alcohol problem and lost custody when Mark was a toddler. She eventually entered rehab and stayed clean for a while. Her first order of business once she was clean was to petition the court to regain custody of Mark.

When sober, Mark's mother was very convincing and promised to adhere to daily AA or NA meetings. As a result, she got Mark back. However, a few months later, the mother relapsed, and Mark was taken from her once again. This continued over and over again for Mark's first thirteen years of life. His mother would relapse, he would go into foster care, and then his mother would get it together and take him home, only to relapse again.

By the time I met Mark, he had had nearly seven placements due to his mother's inability to stay sober and clean. He had been living in a very loving foster home for over a year. In fact, I found out this foster family had started proceedings to adopt Mark. They loved him, and according to Mark, he liked living with them. "It's a normal family. They're good to me," he would tell me.

Unfortunately, Mark's mother again petitioned the court for custody of Mark. He would have to testify in court for the first time and be interviewed by the judge. He was nervous, and I told him, "The judge will likely ask you if you want to stay with your foster family or go back with your mother. What are you going to say?"

His reply was, "I want to go back to my mother."

I was surprised and somewhat perplexed and could not resist adding my thoughts. "But Mark, I know you love your mother, but she has disappointed you so many times before. I hope this time she will stay clean, but there is a strong possibility she will relapse again. I want you to seriously consider that you have a loving foster-care family that wants to adopt you. You said you care for them too, and they are good to you. Do you want to risk losing all that for the chance that your mother might disappoint you again?"

Mark nodded, appearing to fully agree and comprehend my argument. He paused for what seemed forever and then concluded, "But she's my mother."

Mark did go back to his mother. I never found out if it lasted this time, as I was assigned to a new facility. I'm not a betting man, but the odds did not appear to be good.

Teddy the Terror

Teddy was a six-year-old with a serious behavior problem even in a program for elementary school students with behavior problems. He would verbally or physically attack other students at the drop of a hat. Staff members were targets as well. He spent more time in the "quiet room" than in the classroom.

I remember the first day I met him. It was my first day at a program for emotionally behaviorally involved elementary school students. As I exited my car, trying to look as professional as I could, I unknowingly entered the building through the back door closest to the parking lot. Teddy was the first person I saw as I was making my way to the office to sign in.

Teddy was a handsome child, and upon seeing him, I said, "Good morning."

He looked at me with glaring eyes and responded, "Go to hell." That reassured me I was at the right school.

Teddy was one of my regulars, as I was called to intervene in his classroom nearly every day, often more than once. Finally, we had to call in the district psychiatrist, a man I knew well from my days working with him at the state psychiatric hospital. Born in India, Dr. S was the most knowledgeable and insightful medical professional I have ever had the pleasure to work with. I usually accompanied him to parent meetings to translate colloquial American expressions he was unfamiliar with. He spoke the King's English—eloquent, but a disadvantage in most family interventions.

Dr. S decided we needed to speak with Teddy's family and try to get as much background information as we could in hopes of understanding Teddy better.

The invitation went out to the whole family. When the time arrived, there was a solitary figure, Teddy's mother. Dr. S began, "Thank you for coming in today. We were anticipating the appearance of the entirety of Teddy's family as well. Was Teddy's father unable to make this appointment?"

The mother replied, "Yes."

"May I ask why?" Dr. S responded.

"Because he's in jail."

"May I ask the circumstances of his incarceration?"

"You mean how he got there?"

"Yes."

"Well, he got into a bar fight two years ago and killed the guy he was fighting with. He's doing ten to fifteen for second-degree manslaughter."

"Oh I see. And what about Teddy's grandfather? Is Teddy close to him?"

"He's dead."

"May I ask the cause of death?" Dr. S asked.

"Well, he killed his wife, Teddy's grandmother, and then committed suicide last year."

I looked at Dr. S and he looked at me and we both knew in an instant that this was not going to be an easy fix. You can argue the effects of environment or the possibility of a genetic predisposition toward aggressive behavior, but in any event, Teddy was Teddy, and whatever the cause, the need to address Teddy's anger issues remained. Teddy remained one of my regulars.

Eddie's New Year's Eve

After the holiday break one winter after the students returned to class Eddie one of the students I counseled in an elementary school arrived for our scheduled session.

"How was your holiday?" I asked.

"Good."

"Did you celebrate on New Year's Eve?"

"Yes, my parents had a party."

"Did you stay up to see the year change and watch it on TV?"

"Yes, and then my dad and his friends went outside and started shooting their guns up in the air."

"WHAT?"

"Sure, everybody does that."

"No, I don't think so. I don't."

"Why not?"

"Because I don't own a gun and if I did I would probably hit the house next to mine."

Eddie lived in a rural area of Long Island and his family originated from down south. Apparently, where he had previously lived, shooting guns up in the air is a custom in his rural town and his father continued the practice up north, encouraging his buddies to do the same.

And I thought shooting off firecrackers on New Year's would get me in trouble as a kid.

Timmy's Story

Timmy was a sixteen-year-old high school student in a program for emotionally disturbed students. However, Timmy had more than the usual set of challenges. Timmy was also legally blind, had ADHD, was mildly intellectually disabled, had gross motor limitations, and had a severe receptive language learning disability.

I liked Timmy immensely. If nothing else, he was an interesting person and rather funny. He never felt sorry for himself and did his best to succeed academically, but this was a steep hill to climb, to be sure. He barely passed his classes and often got in trouble for leaving his classroom without permission. Timmy and I spent a great deal of time together.

When I first met Timmy early in the school year, I engaged in some small talk and tried to elicit some background information to get to know him better, from his perspective. I always preferred to hear from the student first, rather than read his chart, so I would not be influenced by the reports that existed in the past. I believe each student deserves to be heard, devoid of their past, and thus I can build my own objective picture of each student I work with.

Timmy was well aware of his cognitive and behavioral limitations and, despite his best efforts, often did not succeed to the level of his peers. Near the end of our second session and before I saw his chart, Timmy said to me, "You know why I'm the way I am?"

I truly didn't know at this point and told him, "No, Timmy. What do you mean?"

He replied, "I am the way I am because my mother was a crack addict."

Not sure whether to believe his assertion, later that day, I went to the student files and carefully read his background from birth to the present time. I was not shocked but was still saddened to see he was 100 percent correct. He had been born a crack-addicted baby, and his mother lost custody soon after birth. Timmy was put in foster care and, at five years old, was adopted by a warm and caring family who gave him all the love any family could bestow to any child. Early on, they told him he was adopted, and the family made sure he knew he was chosen by them to be with them, and they never regretted it.

As Timmy grew, he realized he was different than all the other kids in school. He would ask his mother, "Why am I different than everybody?"

His mother tried to downplay the question and told Timmy that no child is good at everything. But Timmy wanted to know why he was no good at *anything*. After months and years of trying to avoid the inevitable, and perhaps frustrated for Timmy as well as herself, Timmy's mother uttered the words Timmy needed to know, and perhaps it came as no surprise to him by then. His mother blurted out, "Because your mother was a crack addict and you were born crack-addicted."

Timmy eventually graduated from high school with a diploma of completion, not worth much in the job market. I had the pleasure of giving him the Perseverance Award at his graduation, and there was not a dry eye in the auditorium, including mine, when he came up to receive his award.

I don't know what happened to Timmy. He was not capable of ever living totally independently. I only hope he was able to find his place in society with a family or agency that provides community residences to those who do not have the ability to live totally independently.

Donna's Many Daddies

Donna was a ten-year-old girl who lived with her mother. Donna never knew her biological father as he took off before she was born. She was scheduled for a reevaluation through her district, and I was assigned to do the evaluation.

During the course of a full comprehensive evaluation, I use a multitude of measures from academic, intellectual, socially adaptive, and project testing, more commonly known as personality testing. To be fair, even some in my field dislike personality testing and refuse to use it or attempt to understand it. A colleague whom I admired greatly referred to personality tests as "bullshit." Now, I, of course, did not share his assumption and, over the years, have found these tests to be quite valuable in understanding my students better and gaining insight into potential issues that need to be explored.

What many in the field of psychology do not fully comprehend is that these tests really only reveal how the individual is feeling at the time of testing. They are not a predictor of the future and rarely reveal past events accurately. In my experience, less than 5 percent of psychologists really know how to apply these testing instruments correctly.

During my testing of Donna, I had my suspicions that there was trauma in her life. It was a gut feeling, and I had no hard evidence that anything was certain. I certainly did not have any evidence to call CPS. I asked an experienced social worker at the program whom I knew well to interview Donna to see if she would reveal anything without putting any words in her mouth.

Despite her best efforts, my friend could not find any issue raised by Donna. I then asked the school nurse to see if Donna showed any suspicious marks on her body or would confide any issue of concern. Again, nothing came back to report.

Unbeknownst to me at the time, Donna's mother had many short-term relationships with male friends that would move in. As bad as that was, the mother insisted that Donna call each of these men "daddy." Now, you can imagine a Russian roulette of strange "daddies" entering Donna's life, only to see them leave after a few months until a new "daddy" would move in. There was more than a good chance that one of these "daddies" was not acting daddy-like.

About three weeks later, Donna came home to find her mother engaged in a screaming tirade with the daddy of the month. In front of Donna, this man pulled out a knife and stabbed her mother repeatedly. Donna ran to a neighbor's house and they called the police. Unfortunately, it was not soon enough for Donna's mother. She was murdered in front of her daughter.

Now, I can't say for certain if this "daddy" was the one that perhaps could have been inappropriately interfering with Donna, but the damage had been done. Donna was taken in by her aunt, but her life was never the same again. How does anyone ever get over watching their mother murdered in front of their eyes?

Bike-Riding Brian

Brian was a twelve-year-old boy who lived at home with his mother and her new boyfriend. Like many who deal with similar issues, he had a difficult time adjusting to this new man in his mother's life. However, his feelings were especially problematic. Brian would refuse to go home and stayed out late at night to avoid seeing this man in his house.

One day, a student from Brian's class came to me and told me in confidence that he was in his mother's car coming home last night and saw Brian riding his bike nearly at midnight on the main street of his town. Not initially believing the student, I was able to ascertain that the story was true when other students reported the same scenario. In addition, this was occurring on a regular basis, even on school nights.

I interviewed Brian in my office and began my inquiry. "Brian, you're not going to believe it, but one of the teachers said they saw you riding your bike on Main Street at midnight one day this week. [I did not want to rat out his fellow students.] Isn't that the craziest thing you ever heard?"

Brian responded, "No. That's true."

"It's true? Why?"

"Because I hate my mother's boyfriend, and I won't go home if he's in the house."

"But Brian, you can't be riding your bike on Main Street at midnight. That's very dangerous, and you need to get your sleep if you are going to do well in school."

"I'm not going home if that bastard is there."

Later, I called the mother after Brian left my office. "Mrs. B," I began. "You're not going to believe this, but Brian told me he was riding his bike on Main Street at midnight last night and that it wasn't the first time. Isn't that the most ridiculous story you ever heard?"

"No, it's true."

"It's true?"

"Yes, he doesn't get along with my boyfriend."

"I realize that, Mrs. B, but you must realize that Brian needs to be home and that riding his bike at midnight down Main Street can be very dangerous for someone his age, never mind that he needs his sleep."

"Well, I can't control him."

I had no choice but to call CPS, who then called the police to intervene. With CPS present, they told the mother that she could not allow her son to be out at midnight at his age on a bicycle, especially on a school night. But his mother repeated what she had said before. "I can't control him."

The police then grew indignant. "Listen, lady, this is your kid. This guy is your boyfriend. You have to make a choice. Is it your son or this boyfriend?"

The mother then made her choice: she chose the boyfriend. Brian wound up in foster care. He concluded I was the one responsible for him leaving his house and would not speak to me again. But I had no choice. Hopefully, one day, he will realize I had his best interest at heart.

Four-Letter-Word Freddy

Freddy was a five-year-old with a vocabulary like a drunken sailor. His use of the F word flowed as quickly from his mouth as water from a fountain. Despite their best efforts, teachers could not get a grasp on his verbiage. He was becoming very disruptive in a kindergarten class where the other students would laugh or try to correct him by saying, "That's a bad word," but to no avail. Freddy's teacher said we needed to speak with his parents, and a meeting was arranged.

Freddy's mother and father arrived at the agreed-upon day and time. Freddy's teacher and I were present. His teacher opened the meeting. "Mr. and Mrs. F, we are very concerned about Freddy's inappropriate language. His use of the F word causes much disruption in class and some of his classmates are starting to repeat these words he uses. We have tried, but we are unable to get him to stop or at least reduce his use of the F word. Is there any assistance you can offer to help us with this issue with Freddy?"

The father responded, "I don't know where he gets this fucking language from. We don't talk like this at fucking home. I don't know what's wrong with this fucking kid. This is a fucking mystery to me. Can anybody explain to me why he uses this fucking language?

I glanced over at Freddy's teacher and had to literally bite my lower lip to keep from bursting out laughing. We knew in an instant that this was not an issue that was going to be solved that day. Or any day in the near future. We could work with Freddy to the best of our ability, but we were unlikely to change his father.

Jose Rodriguez

Jose Rodriguez (*not his real name, but relevant to this story*) was a student in ninth grade who was in a program for those with an intellectual disability. "Intellectual disability" is the more appropriate term for the previously derogatory descriptive "mental retardation."

Jose seemed to be a typical student. He was a handsome Hispanic-looking youngster and he spoke English with a heavy Spanish accent, but his verbiage was grammatically correct. He certainly did not exhibit any significant learning problems.

Jose was scheduled to be reevaluated by his district, and I was scheduled to administer this evaluation. However, a few days before the date of testing, I went to check out his file and review the evaluation conducted three years previously. A bilingual school psychologist that I did not know from his past program had administered the Spanish version of the intelligence test. Most of the widely used evaluations have versions of their test in other languages for English language learners. This is the same test that I administer in English and involves verbally responding to different types of general questions and vocabulary, along with some visual-motor activities.

Not being fluent in the language, I would not be able to administer the test in Spanish. However, I had my suspicions about the previous test that had diagnosed Jose as intellectually disabled when the test was administered in Spanish.

The following day I met with Jose again. I asked him if he recalled a test a lady gave him that involved answering different types of questions and puzzles. He said he did remember. I asked him if he recalled that the test was in Spanish. He again said, "Yes."

I then asked, "Jose, how well do you speak and understand Spanish?"

His reply: "Not so good."

I then quickly responded, "Jose, why didn't you tell this lady you don't understand and speak Spanish well?"

His answer was very logical: "I thought it was a Spanish test."

Jose, who had a Hispanic name, appeared Hispanic and spoke English with a Spanish accent, was given the test in Spanish. The previous school psychologist looking and listening to Jose assumed that Spanish was Jose's primary language. A major faux-pas. Jose was a first-generation American whose parents came from South America. His parents spoke very little English, and he learned to speak English with a heavy Spanish accent. Just like the geographic part of the country you have grown up in, you may speak English with a Brooklyn, Bostonian, Southern, or Midwestern accent.

I then administered the same test, but this time in Jose's primary language, English. The result: Jose was of average intelligence. My immediate step was to meet with the principal of the program and inform her of the news.

"We have to get Jose back to district, and it needs to be done yesterday." Jose was sent back a few short days later to his district, from which he should never have been removed.

Coffee-Cake Charlie

When I first started working in a psychiatric hospital, some of the patients would try to con me into sneaking in beer, drugs, or other types of contraband that would have resulted in me losing my job, license, and likely getting arrested.

I recall one patient asking me to buy him a large coffee cake that was sold at the nearby bakery selling expired cakes on dollar Thursdays. Thinking that this was a safe request, and knowing that the dessert options on an inpatient psychiatric ward are limited, I agreed. The patient gave me his dollar, and I obliged and picked him up the large dollar coffee cake on my lunch break. The patient thanked me for his purchase and I returned to my office.

Later that day, I heard the nurses complaining that Charlie was taking money from the other residents. What Charlie had done was carefully cut up the cake into twelve small pieces and sold them to the other patients for a dollar each. I later found out he had a number of staff that he conned into doing the same. He ran a brisk business. His options included cookies, muffins, soda, and instant coffee that he sold by the teaspoon. He was clearing over $200 a week.

I decided to keep quiet, but that was the last time I bought coffee cake for Charlie.

SlimFast Steve

I should have learned my lesson from Charlie, but six months after the coffee-cake incident, one of my patients, Steve, a fairly big man, heard a commercial about a product called SlimFast on TV and wanted to try it to lose weight. SlimFast comes in powdered form. You add a scoop to low-fat milk and mix it as a meal substitute.

I was reluctant, but Steve pleaded with me that he really wanted to lose weight and be healthier. He gave me his money, and foolishly, I purchased the can of SlimFast for him the following day. He thanked me and disappeared into the bathroom. Five minutes later, he returned with an empty can.

I asked him, "Where is the SlimFast?"

His reply: "I mixed it with water and drank it."

"All of it? Steve, there were thirty servings in that can. You were only supposed to take one scoop and mix it with milk once a day!"

He then said, "But I wanna slim *real fast*."

I had no option but to report my indiscretion to the head nurse, who scolded me for being so naïve and promised me she would keep an eye on Steve as he was sure to be constipated. Later that week, the same nurse reassured me that *everything came out all right*. That was the last time I ever was conned by a patient again.

Window Voices

I was conducting a group therapy session at the psychiatric hospital on an all-male adult ward. Attendance was optional, but those who attended got coffee and a snack. That usually brought out *I'll never go to group therapy* guys. On this particular day, all seemed to be going well in group. I did not bring up any controversial issues. Just basic chitchat.

I then noticed one of my regulars got up from the group. This was not a concern, as the patients were allowed to get up and stretch their legs or, if need be, could make a quick bathroom stop. As the patient proceeded over to the window area on the ward, I continued with my group. Suddenly, and without any warning or provocation, this patient put his fist through the window with full force.

Nurses were called; doctors were paged. There was blood everywhere. I applied pressure to the patient's arm with a towel and waited for the rest of the staff to assist and take over. After the smoke had settled and the patient was returned from the infirmary with twenty fresh stitches on his arm, I went to find out what had happened.

I said, in my most professional voice, "What the hell was that!"

He replied, "I broke the window."

I replied, "I know you broke the window. I was there! Why did you break it?"

"I had to."

"You had to? What do you mean?" I asked.

"The voices in my head told me to break the window." (I know, I should have realized. This was a psychiatric hospital.)

I continued, "But that didn't mean you *had* to break the window just because the voices told you to do it." (I thought that was a very logical statement at the time.)

His reply was apparently just as logical. "No, you don't understand. It was the only way I could get the voices to stop."

Again, I should have realized where I was and that he and my remaining patients were not here for a summer vacation. Lesson learned.

Where's My Therapist?

On occasion, psychologists cover for each other if someone is sick or on vacation. The administrator in my building asked me to cover for a colleague and conduct his group therapy session one day. This particular ward of thirty men was not one I normally interacted with. However, they had seen me in the building and were somewhat familiar with me.

I began by asking the men to gather on the day hall, voluntarily, of course, so we could begin. I introduced myself and said I would be filling in for their usual psychologist. Barely two minutes into my discussion, I heard a loud crash, simultaneously knocking me off my chair. I blacked out for a few minutes and when I came to, I was lying down.

The head nurse looked at me and said, "We need to get you to the hospital!"

"What happened?"

She handed me a mirror. My forehead had been cut open and there was a three-inch gap where my skin had separated. It looked like I had been scalped. Plus, I could barely walk as the garbage can that had been thrown at my head had also dislocated a disc in my back. I later found out one of the patients in the group came to the conclusion that I not only had replaced his favorite therapist but had killed him as well.

I was rushed to the nearest medical facility from the psychiatric hospital and carried into the emergency room, bleeding profusely from my forehead. The intake nurse told me they were trying to page the plastic surgeon, who was just on his way out. Luckily for me, they literally caught him on the way out the door. He looked at me and said, "I need to get you stitched up."

I quickly agreed, but there was a catch. The surgeon could not anesthetize my forehead as the skin on one's forehead is so thin and next to the skull. He said, "This is how it's going to go. You can yell, you can scream, but don't move."

Twenty stitches were slowly and carefully applied to my forehead to reattach the skin that had separated. I could feel the surgeon's needle entering my forehead and the silk that slid through the small incisions he had made. Fifteen painful minutes of "Ow, ow ow," and a couple of "goddamns" and other profanity-laced words later, it was done. He then circled my head with enough gauze and bandages so that I looked like the genie from *Aladdin*. My head now appeared twice the normal size. The Elephant Man had nothing on me.

That would have been the end of the story had it not been that I was scheduled to begin my first introduction to psychology class at the local community college. Not wanting to miss the first class despite my appearance, being barely able to walk with a cane, and being drugged up with painkillers, I must have been an awesome sight.

I walked into a full class and announced, barely coherently: "Will come to in tro duct ion of sy col o g." Four students ran out screaming; the rest packed their bags. The remainder dropped the class. Problem solved!

Will the Real Jesus Christ Please Stand Up?

Many patients on the inpatient ward I worked on had serious delusions. And when people have delusions, they can be pretty unusual. It just so happened on this ward I had four patients who all proclaimed to be Jesus Christ. Now, whatever your religious affiliation, I only know of one historically. So I was inspired to have a group counseling session with all four JCs. I figured they would all realize the error of their ways and come to some lucid comprehension, with my assistance, of course.

As the four gentlemen were seated in a circle, I asked each patient to introduce himself.

Patient 1: "My name is Jesus Christ."

Patient 2: "My name is Jesus Christ."

Patient 3: "My name is Jesus Christ."

Patient 4: "My name is Jesus Christ."

It was like the old game show from the sixties, To Tell the Truth, where one of the three contestants was the real famous person and the others were imposters. Except here, they were all telling the truth. What happened next resembled a tag-wrestling match and free-for-all.

"What? You lying bastard, I am the real Jesus Christ."

"No you're not. I am the Messiah."

"No, I am the real Jesus Christ."

"You're all nuts, 'cause I am the real Jesus Christ, and I'll teach you for saying that I'm not."

"Help, help!" I yelled out. "I need help! I have a situation here."

Not my first or last bad idea.

Epilogue

It took many years to realize that, as much as I had hoped to accomplish, I could not cure or fix everyone I came in contact with. But that doesn't mean you should stop trying. Professional therapist or not, each person has the power to change someone else's life. I would be the first to admit that you don't need to seek professional help for most of life's emotional problems. All most of us really need is a good listener. If you are a good listener, you are as valuable as any therapist on earth. Keep doing what you are doing. You *do* make a difference.

I stumbled upon this short story, and it helped me through the difficult times in my career. I made some personal changes.

The Old Man and the Starfish

My variation of the original story by Loren Eiseley

There was a young man who used to go to the ocean every day as part of his morning workout. He had a habit of running on the beach every morning before he went to work. Early one morning, he was running along the shore after a big storm had passed and found the beach littered with starfish as far as the eye could see, stretching in both directions.

Off in the distance, the young man noticed an old man. He watched as the old man picked up objects and threw them into the sea. The young man came closer and called out, "Hey, old man, what are you doing?"

The old man looked up and replied, "Throwing starfish into the ocean. The tide has washed them up onto the beach and they can't return to the sea by themselves. They can't survive long out of the ocean. They will die unless I throw them back into the water."

The young man replied, "But there must be hundreds of starfish on this beach, old man. You're wasting your time. You won't really make much of a difference."

The old man bent down and continued picking up yet another starfish which he threw back into the ocean. Then he turned to the young man and said, "It made a difference to that one!"

About the Author

Dr. Karahalis has over thirty-five years' experience as a certified school psychologist and is a licensed mental health counselor specializing in individuals with special needs, in particular intellectual disability, autism spectrum disorder, and schizophrenia, as well as nonspecific cognitive, emotional, and physical challenges from preschool through adulthood.

Dr. Karahalis' experiences include working for nonprofit agencies, government, developmental and psychiatric facilities, and public and private school districts. He also has an active consulting practice. Dr. Karahalis is an adjunct professor of psychology with over thirty years of collegiate service at private and public community colleges.

Dr. Karahalis' experiences include working closely with schools, students, and families, providing services to pre- and post-graduate special-needs students in implementing coherent individualized education and service plans. These include comprehensive cognitive, adaptive, projective, and autism specialty evaluations as needed, as well as individual and group counseling, crisis intervention, and parent and staff development training programs.

Dr. Karahalis has five degrees, including psychology, school psychology, child psychology, and educational leadership. Dr. Karahalis is married with three children and lives in Long Island, NY.